Hooray!
It's Halloween today!
I put on my pointy hat and broom.
What a scary witch costume!

I can't wait to go out and trick-or-treat.
I'll get some yummy candy to eat!

There are goblins and ghosts all over my block.

I go to my neighbor's house and knock.

"Trick or treat? Trick or treat! Give me something good to eat!"

A candy corn triangle sure is sweet!

I run up to the second door.
I love candy and I want more!

Mr. Jones answers and I yell,
"Trick or treat? Trick or treat! Give me something good to eat!"

What do I get? I won't tell.
I'll give you a hint—it has a minty smell!

Now it's time for house number three.
I still can't believe this candy is free!

Mrs. Smith answers her doorbell.
Once again, it's time to yell,

"Trick or treat! Trick or treat! Give me something good to eat!"
Mrs. Smith gives me a square caramel!

At the end of the block is house number four.
I walk right up and knock on the door.

"Trick or treat! Trick or treat!
Give me something good to eat!"

I hold out my pumpkin-shaped Halloween jar,
and Mrs. Brown gives me a candy bar.

Halloween candy comes in all shapes and sizes!
Did you find all of the candy prizes?